LOOK OUT FOR BUGS

Jen Prokopowicz

First edition April 2015.

Art direction by Christopher Herndon
Cover by Jen Prokopowicz
Book design by Jen Prokopowicz and Christopher Herndon
Book layout by Brian David Smith

_____

Library of Congress Cataloging-in-Publication Data

Prokopowicz, Jen, author, illustrator.
 Look out for bugs! / by Jen Prokopowicz. -- First edition.
      pages cm
 Audience: Age 5.
 Audience: K to grade 3.
 ISBN 978-1-940052-14-4
1. Insects--Juvenile literature. I. Title.
 QL467.2.P758 2015
 595.7--dc23

                                        2014040182

First hardcover edition ISBN: 978-1-940052-1-44.

Portland, OR
www.craigmorecreations.com

Printed in the United States of America

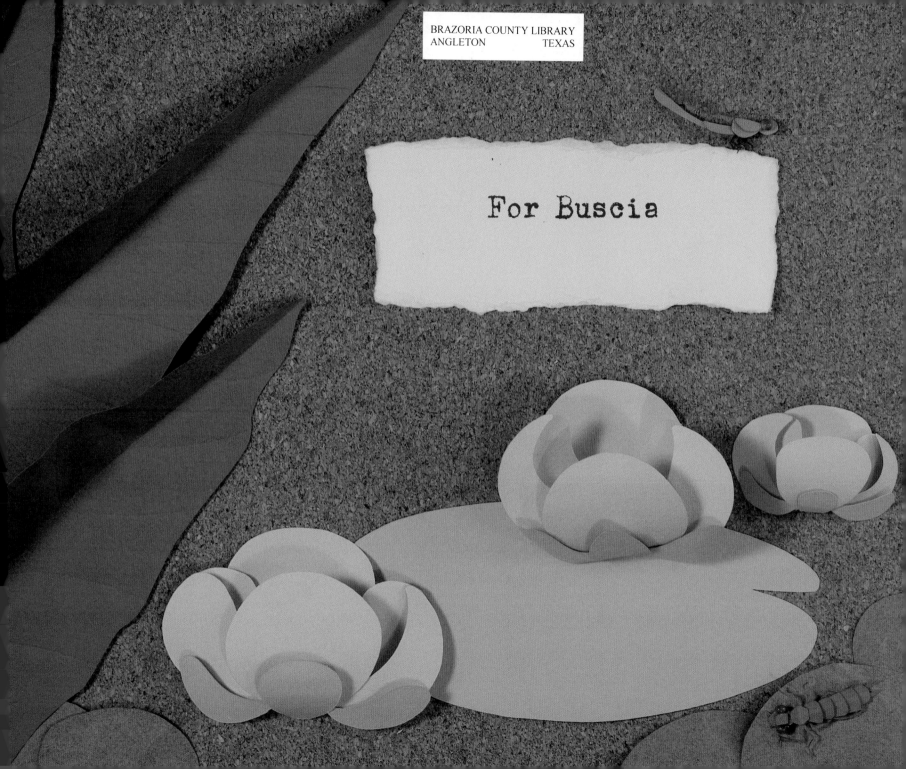

For Buscia

INTRODUCTION

When you go out exploring, you may hear insects chirping
in the bushes, or see them flying through the air, but
did you know that there are even more insects hiding all
around you? Insects have adapted clever camouflage, helping
them match their environment to provide protection from
predators. Many different kinds of animals would love to
make a meal of a small bug.

If you look closely, you may notice all kinds of insects
hiding in plain sight.

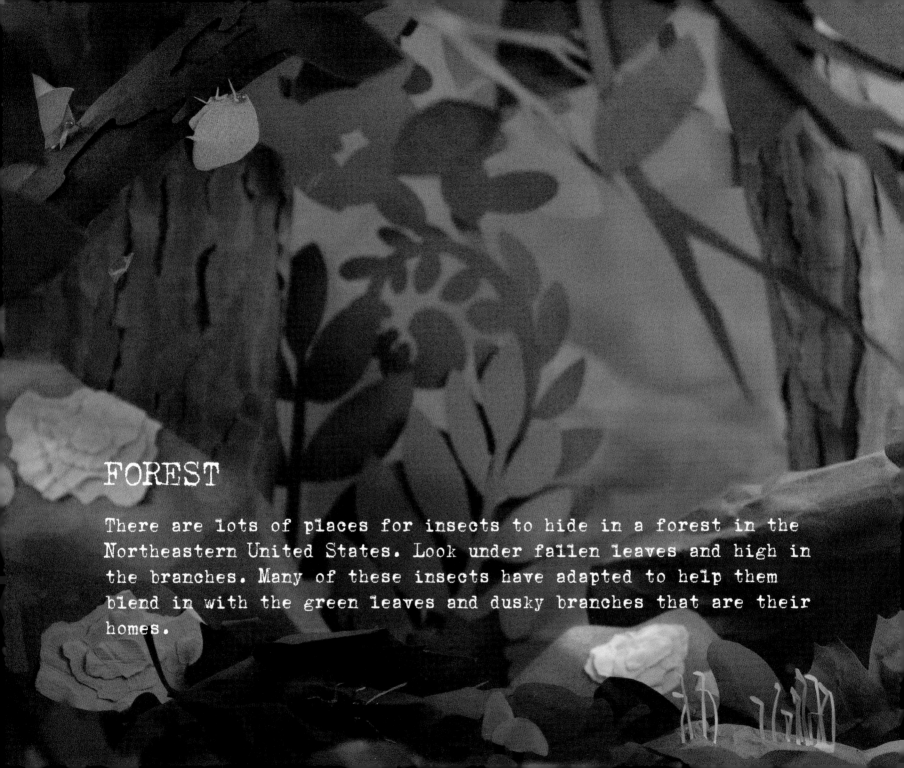

FOREST

There are lots of places for insects to hide in a forest in the Northeastern United States. Look under fallen leaves and high in the branches. Many of these insects have adapted to help them blend in with the green leaves and dusky branches that are their homes.

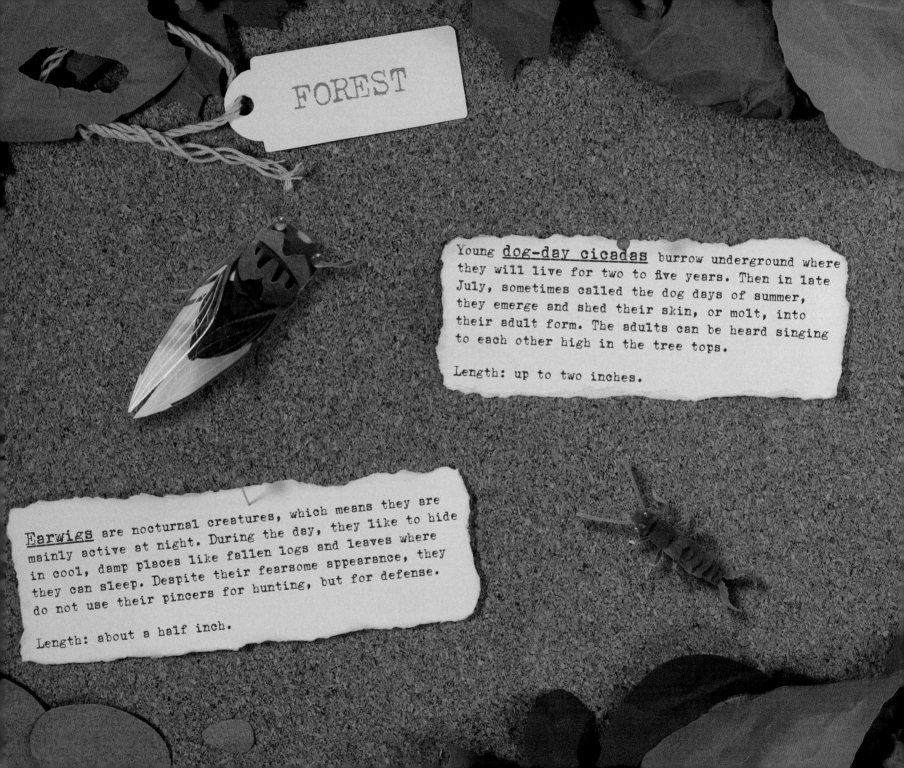

FOREST

Young <u>dog-day cicadas</u> burrow underground where they will live for two to five years. Then in late July, sometimes called the dog days of summer, they emerge and shed their skin, or molt, into their adult form. The adults can be heard singing to each other high in the tree tops.

Length: up to two inches.

<u>Earwigs</u> are nocturnal creatures, which means they are mainly active at night. During the day, they like to hide in cool, damp places like fallen logs and leaves where they can sleep. Despite their fearsome appearance, they do not use their pincers for hunting, but for defense.

Length: about a half inch.

The **yellow garden spider** likes to build its web far from the ground in tall shrubs near open areas. Its delicate web can seem to disappear into the background, but for the bold zigzag pattern it makes in the center.

Length: about a half inch.

Pill bugs live on the ground in cool, shady places. If you disturb one, it may curl into a ball to protect itself. Despite their name and land lubbing lifestyle, they are not insects at all but are more closely related to shrimp and crayfish.

Pill bugs are about a half-inch long.

Buffalo treehoppers perch on woody tree branches. Their shape resembles that of a thorn and they seem to be a part of the branch when they are at rest. They sing in the summer like crickets, but their song is so high pitched that it can't be heard by human ears.

Length: about a half inch.

MARSH

In a marsh in the Southeastern United States you can find a large variety of insects. These insects thrive in the damp, humid environment, and many of them make their nurseries in the water. There are lots of good hiding places in a marsh, and these insects are adapted to make full use of the reeds and tall grass.

MARSH

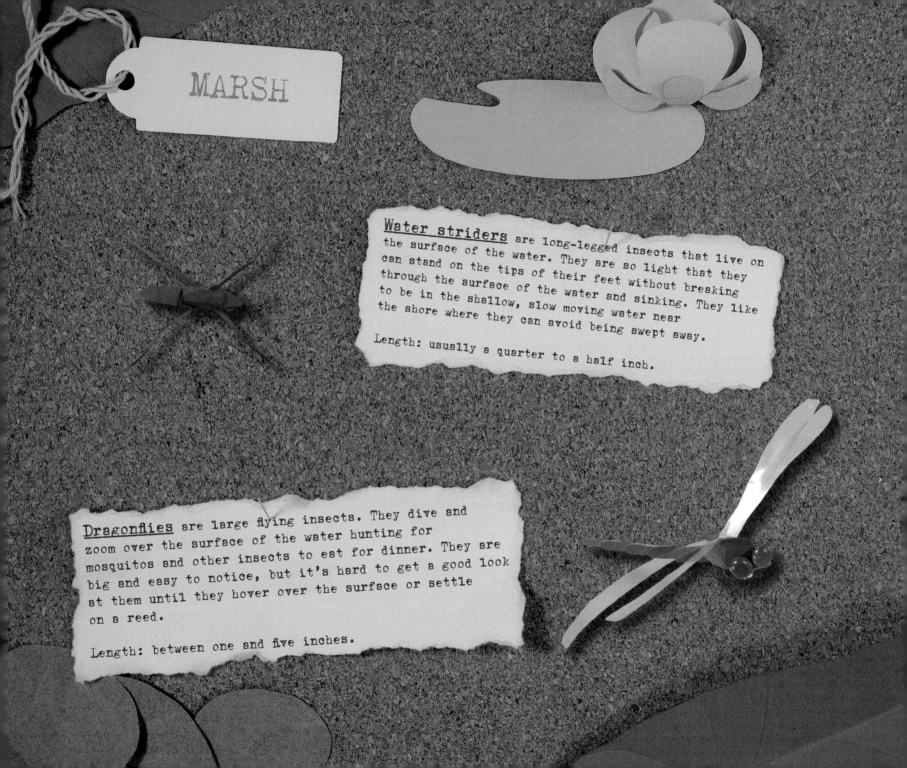

Water striders are long-legged insects that live on the surface of the water. They are so light that they can stand on the tips of their feet without breaking through the surface of the water and sinking. They like to be in the shallow, slow moving water near the shore where they can avoid being swept away.

Length: usually a quarter to a half inch.

Dragonflies are large flying insects. They dive and zoom over the surface of the water hunting for mosquitos and other insects to eat for dinner. They are big and easy to notice, but it's hard to get a good look at them until they hover over the surface or settle on a reed.

Length: between one and five inches.

Damselflies look like tiny dragonflies, but don't be fooled! They are a different species entirely. An easy way to tell them apart, besides their difference in size, is by looking at their wings. A dragonfly holds its wings straight out from its sides when at rest, while a damselfly folds its wings close to its body.

Length: one to two inches.

Mayflies are large, short-lived flying insects. They can spend up to two years in their nymph stage, but only live for one day in their adult form. The nymphs climb out of the water onto reeds or logs where they shed their skin and metamorphose into their adult form.

Length: usually between a half inch and an inch.

Sulfur butterflies like to visit marshes for the mud! Butterflies of all kinds can sometimes be found in groups in a bog sipping nutrients and minerals from the mud that they can't get from flowers. This behavior is known as mud puddling.

Wingspan: up to two inches.

DESERT

The desert is home to many insects, despite the dry and arid climate. While some are active during the day, many are nocturnal and only come out at night. They spend the day tucked into burrows or under rocks away from the sun's rays.

DESERT

Bark scorpions are hardy predators. They are nocturnal, and prefer to spend the hottest parts of the day asleep in cool, dark places like rocky crevices. They have a stinger at the end of their long segmented tails, which they use to paralyze their prey and use for defense.

Length ranges from two to three inches.

Agave weevils can be distinguished from other beetles by their long, beak-like snouts. The adults of this species use their snouts to bore holes into agave plants and drink the sap.

Length: about a half inch.

Carrot beetles are robust little scarabs. They are nocturnal and spend the heat of the day sleeping under cover. At night, they emerge to feed on plants, with a particular preference for tough roots, which they get at by burrowing.

Length: up to an inch and a half.

Cactus bugs live on the prickly pear cactuses on which they feed. They do not have jaws, but instead pierce the tough pads of the cactus with a beak and suck out the juice inside like a straw. They mainly consume the juice from the pads of the cactus and leave the fruit alone. You can tell where they've been by the white blotches they leave behind on the cactus.

Length: about a half inch.

Ironclad beetles are hardy insects that have been known to live for up to ten years, which is a very long time for an insect. They roam around the desert looking for decaying vegetation to eat. They have very tough exoskeletons and are famous for playing dead when disturbed. Their powder blue color comes from a special coating they excrete to protect themselves from the sun.

Length: usually up to an inch.

CREEK

In a slow moving stream in the Midwestern United States, swimming and diving insects make their home. Many of these are nymphs, an immature form of flying aquatic insects that live near the water or spend their entire lives underwater.

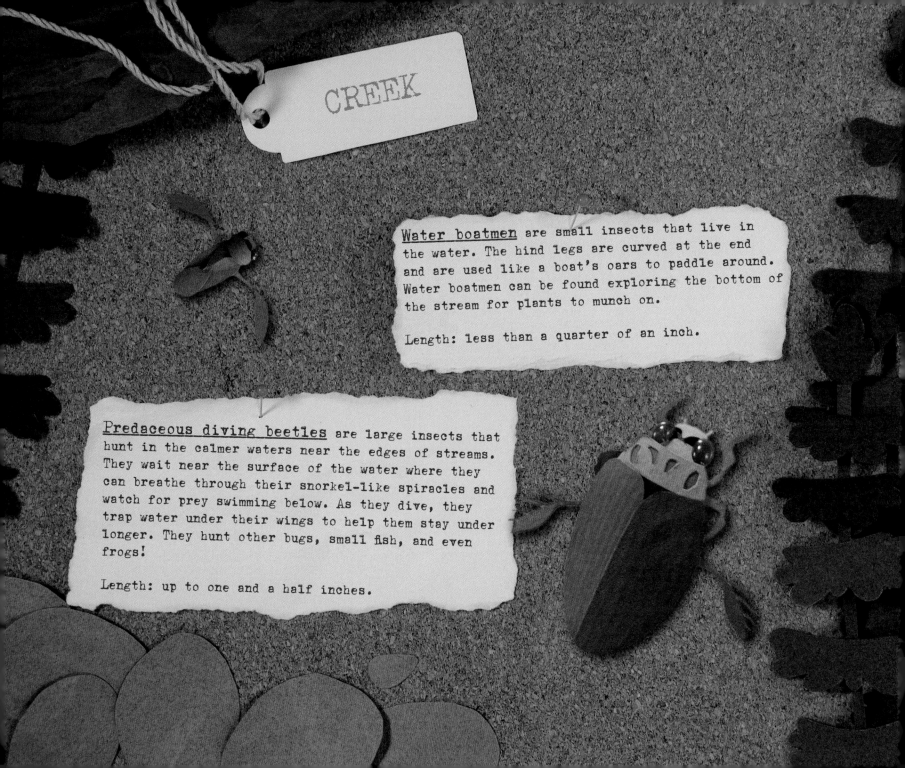

CREEK

Water boatmen are small insects that live in
the water. The hind legs are curved at the end
and are used like a boat's oars to paddle around.
Water boatmen can be found exploring the bottom of
the stream for plants to munch on.

Length: less than a quarter of an inch.

Predaceous diving beetles are large insects that
hunt in the calmer waters near the edges of streams.
They wait near the surface of the water where they
can breathe through their snorkel-like spiracles and
watch for prey swimming below. As they dive, they
trap water under their wings to help them stay under
longer. They hunt other bugs, small fish, and even
frogs!

Length: up to one and a half inches.

Dragonfly nymphs are the immature form of a dragonfly. Dragonflies lay their eggs on underwater plants. The nymphs hatch out and spend about a year underwater hunting for other insects.

Length: usually one to three inches.

Caddisfly larvae are the immature form of a caddisfly. The nymphs spin sticky silk, somewhat like a spider, which they use to build their homes. They attach tiny pieces of gravel together in a tube shape to make a protective case. When it's time to pupate into their adult form, they anchor the case to a rock and close both ends. They will emerge as full grown caddisflies.

The larvae can grow up to a half-inch long.

Water stick insects are stealthy predators. Their twig-like bodies help them to blend in with the stalks of aquatic plants. They hide motionlessly and wait for unsuspecting prey to swim by, then capture their dinner with their specially adapted front legs.

Length: up to two inches.

MEADOW

Walk through a meadow in the West and you may see many insects flying and leaping. Some of these insects drink the nectar of a variety of wildflowers that grow there, while others are effective hunters.

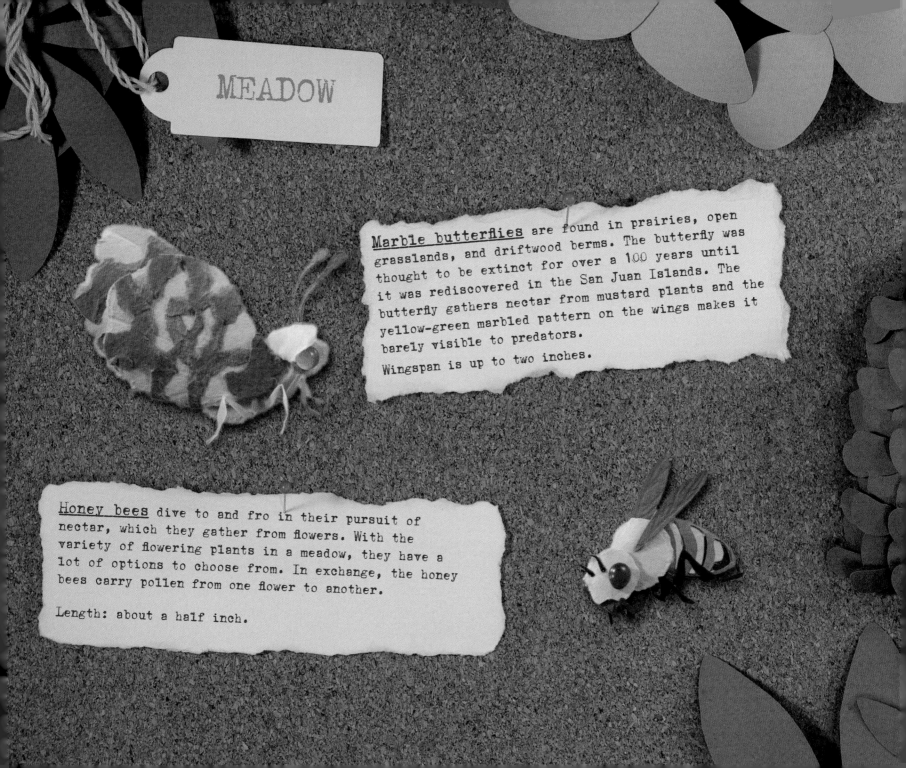

MEADOW

Marble butterflies are found in prairies, open grasslands, and driftwood berms. The butterfly was thought to be extinct for over a 100 years until it was rediscovered in the San Juan Islands. The butterfly gathers nectar from mustard plants and the yellow-green marbled pattern on the wings makes it barely visible to predators.

Wingspan is up to two inches.

Honey bees dive to and fro in their pursuit of nectar, which they gather from flowers. With the variety of flowering plants in a meadow, they have a lot of options to choose from. In exchange, the honey bees carry pollen from one flower to another.

Length: about a half inch.

Red-legged grasshoppers leap among the tall grass. At rest, their green color can help them blend in with the surrounding plants. You might not notice them until you get too close and they leap away from you. Grasshoppers use their wings to extend their jumps, flying in short noisy bursts.

Length: about one inch.

Spittlebugs can be seen jumping from leaf to leaf. Their name comes from the curious behavior displayed in their nymph stage. Young spittlebugs make a frothy foam to hide themselves in what looks like spit! The substance keeps them protected and helps them regulate moisture until it's time to molt into their adult form.

Length: usually about one-eighth of an inch.

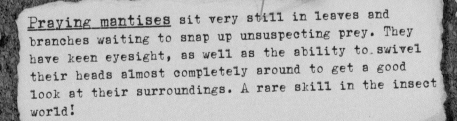

Praying mantises sit very still in leaves and branches waiting to snap up unsuspecting prey. They have keen eyesight, as well as the ability to swivel their heads almost completely around to get a good look at their surroundings. A rare skill in the insect world!

Length: up to seven inches.

YOUR BACKYARD

You don't need to go far to find hiding insects in your backyard. They are all around you! Look closely and see what you can see.

Big fuzzy bumblebees rumble around the garden
in search of nectar. You can tell them apart from
honey bees by their larger size and distinct black
and white stripe pattern. Look carefully for their
pollen baskets, a dusty accumulation of pollen on
their hind legs.

Length: up to one inch.

Ladybugs are beneficial garden helpers. They prey on many
pest insects that would otherwise cause damage to plants.
Ladybugs like to spend the winter together in large
numbers. They gather in protected places like under tree
bark, under leaves, and even between the wood that makes
a window frame.
Length: about half an inch.

Stink bugs are plant eaters that get their name from the smell they produce as a defense when disturbed. They like to enter human habitats to hibernate for the winter. In spring, they often lose their way to the exit and may end up wandering around your home by mistake.

Length: usually about half an inch.

Green lacewings are delicate flying insects. The adults are nocturnal and are often attracted to porch lights. During the day they rest on the leaves and stems of plants where their green coloring helps them hide. They are predators and feed mainly on aphids.

Length: about three quarters of an inch.

Goldenrod crab spiders are tricky ambush predators. They do not use a web for catching prey, but instead hide in flowers and wait for insects to come to them. Camouflage is very important to these little spiders, and they have been known to change their color from yellow to white depending on the color of the flower they are on.

Length: about half an inch.

FOREST

MARSH

DESERT

CREEK

MEADOW

YOUR BACKYARD

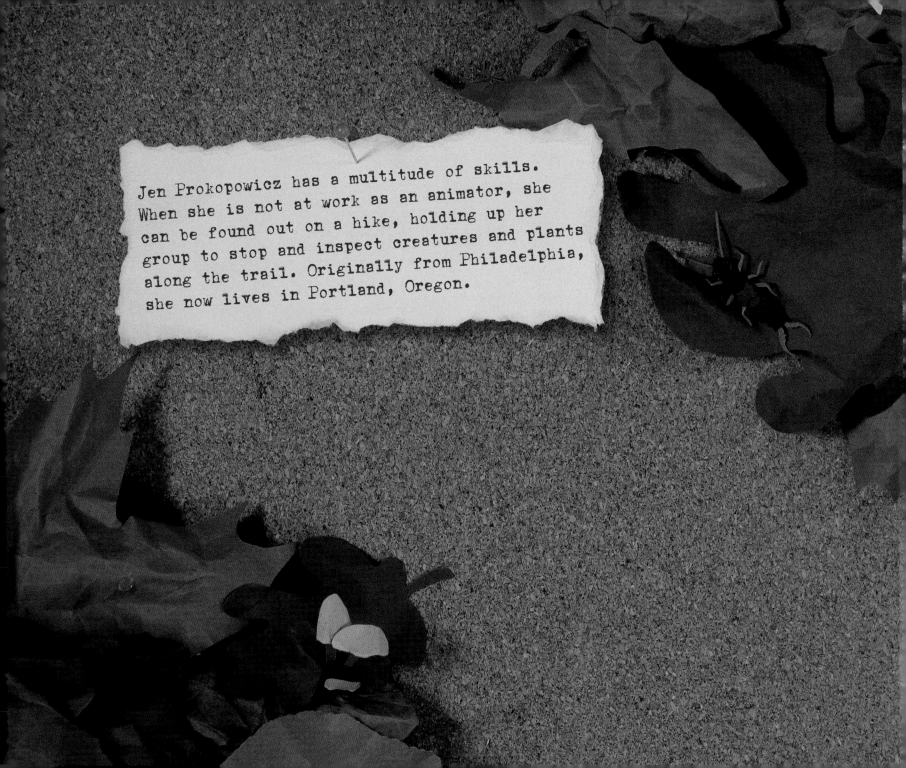

Jen Prokopowicz has a multitude of skills. When she is not at work as an animator, she can be found out on a hike, holding up her group to stop and inspect creatures and plants along the trail. Originally from Philadelphia, she now lives in Portland, Oregon.